The Church Held Hostage

The plight of the small local church

By

Pastor Alfred A. Dingle Sr.

The Church Held Hostage

The plight of the small local church

By

Pastor Alfred A. Dingle Sr.

AD Ministries

All Scriptures quotes from the King James Version

Cover design and drawing by Pastor Alfred A. Dingle Sr.

Order this book online at www.trafford.com
or email orders@trafford.com

Most Trafford titles are also available at major online book retailers.

Printed in Victoria, BC, Canada.

ISBN: 978-1-4269-3234-2 (soft)

Library of Congress Control Number: 2010905423

*Our mission is to efficiently provide the world's finest, most comprehensive book publishing
service, enabling every author to experience success. To find out how to publish your
book, your way, and have it available worldwide, visit us online at www.trafford.com*

Trafford rev. 7/23/2010

 www.trafford.com

North America & international
toll-free: 1 888 232 4444 (USA & Canada)
phone: 250 383 6864 ♦ fax: 812 355 4082

Acknowledgements

To: Rev. Simon Dingle Sr. and Evangelist Laverne Dingle for your love, prayers and support.

Evangelist Inez Branch for your prayers, encouragement and support in my ministry.

To: Pastor Willie W. Wilson for his tutelage and giving me the opportunity to exercise my calling and my gifts.

To: Bishop and Evangelist Harris and family, grandpa and grandma for your love and prayers.

To Pastor Milton "Pop" Byrd, who adopted me as his son in the ministry, for your support in my ministry.

To all the pastors such as Rev. L. Pendleton, Rev. Dr. Perry Simmons Jr., Rev. William H. Rutherford, Rev. Joe D. McClain, the late Sammy Lee Hawkins, Rev. Bennett Johnson and all that are too numerous to name, who planted seeds of encouragement into my ministry.

To the Singing Pastors of Piscataway NJ who I enjoy singing with. You all have been a great blessing to me.

To my children: Alfred Alonzo Jr.; Clarysha Nate`, Christopher Allen, and grandchildren, Ta`lik and Naasir

To all my sisters, Darlene, in South Carolina, Laura Ethel, Van Dora, Patricia, Sandra, Rosa and Lanette, in NJ and my brother, Minister Simon Dingle Jr., also in South Carolina, nieces and nephews.

Dedications

This book is dedicated to all my family and friends who prayed for me and encouraged me throughout my life and my ministry.

This is also dedicated to all the pastors and churches with small congregations who share a like struggle. My prayer is that we will all increase in strength and in members that we may fulfill our obligation within the body of Christ and decrease our hindrances.

Also in the memory of my mother, Vera L. Dingle, my grandfather, Rev. Sheppard Dingle, the founder and pastor of the St. Phillips Baptist Church in Russellville So. Carolina.

Also to my grandmother, Evangelist Laura Dingle in St. Stephens South Carolina who, thanks be to God, is still with us today.

Special Thanks

I want to first give praise and thanks to God my heavenly Father and my Lord and Savior Jesus Christ for looking beyond my faults and supplying my needs. I thank Him for the blessings and the gifts He entrusted and bestowed upon me through the Holy Spirit. To God is the glory forever and ever.

Next, I want to thank my Dad, Rev. Simon Dingle Sr., and Pastor of the Central Baptist Church in Jersey City NJ, and Momma Laverne Dingle for their support and encouragement in my music and preaching ministry. I thank my Dad for being an example for me in writing. I would not have envisioned the Lord taking me this far, but the Lord knew. Many things I did not understand when I was young but I'm grateful for my upbringing. Dad I love you. Also I thank God for Momma Verne for all her love and support. She is a very special blessing. Momma Verne I love you.

Also to my dear departed mother, Vera L. Dingle, I wish you were here to witness what the Lord is doing with your baby boy. I love you and miss you very, very much.

To the Memorial Baptist Church where I have served as pastor for over 12 years, I thank God for you all. There are many who left us for a host of reasons. But I thank God for the people who stayed through and during many of our struggles. I truly believe that God is preparing us for His mighty movement. I appreciate the opportunity to serve as your pastor. Memorial, I love you all.

To my grandmother, Evangelist Laura Dingle who has been and continues to be a spiritual rock in our family, my prayer is that our God will continue to keep her strong.

To all my family in South Carolina and abroad who are too numerous to mention by name, thank you all for being who you are to me.

To a very special friend who has become a big part of my life, Vanessa. You have given me the extra boost in life that I needed to complete this project.

Also to my son in the ministry Rev. Derry Thomas and his wife, thank you for having my back in the recent storms in the church.

Next to my mother - in - law, Evangelist Inez Branch who has been a great supporter of my ministry from the very beginning, thank you for your words of challenge, confidence and encouragement. Also to my late father - in - law, Bunyan Branch, I miss you too.

To Bishop Harris and Mother Harris, grandpa and grandma, and the entire Harris family, thank you all for your prayers.

Contents

Introduction

We are told by scientists that there are no two snowflakes identical to each other. The actuality of this scientific analysis is difficult to comprehend because of the enormous volume of snowflakes that fall at one time. In other words, to solidify that this is in fact true, one must either take the time to go through an exhaustive investigative study to examine each flake, or take someone's word for it. Whether we stand upon the analysis of scientific discoveries or not, I have come to recognize that snowflakes have certain similarities and characteristics that are identical in nature. They all are made with water, can only survive in cold weather, fall from the sky, etc. In my observation of some churches,

I've noticed that this analogy can also apply to churches. Although I believe it to be true that there are no two churches that are identical, there are certainly many similarities. It is not the differences of churches and denominations that we will focus our primary attention, but the similarities that encompass the difficulties of the small local church that we want to place our focus. For in any and in every organization and institution there will be issues. We must be reminded that there are forces outside the church warring against us. Ephesians 6: 12; "For we wrestle not against flesh and blood, but against principalities, against powers, against the rulers of the darkness of this world, against spiritual wickedness in high places." These forces at times can be and are merciless and treacherous. But we are informed through the word of God in Romans 8:37 "Nay, in all these things we are more than conquerors through Him that loved us." It is not just the outside forces attacking the church that presents obstacles to the church that we want to emphasize and recognize, but primarily the inside forces that corrodes and erodes the infrastructure of the small church. It is hard enough dealing with trouble from the outside of the church, but it's worst when those who should work for the well being of the church become part of the problem and not part of the solution. Whether they are greater in the larger and "mega churches" or not, I can't say. I can only speak from my personal experience as pastor of a small congregation. There are circumstances in life that we have little or no control. While we will consider this matter and manner later, we want to first focus on the situations and circumstances in life that people claim to have no control over. Although people will use these situations and circumstances to hold the small church hostage, it's the areas of life people are untruthful about concerning their **so called trouble** that we will examine. It's these so called troubles people use as their excuse to avoid church responsibilities. I'm convinced that it's the circumstances in life that people have a reasonable amount of, or a lot of control over, that holds the small church hostage. Don't misunderstand me. The small church transcends structural size and membership enrollment. For it is very possible for a large congregation to be small. That is to say small in ministry, small in mind and small in faith. Whatever and wherever the movement of God in the Holy Spirit is hindered, stunted and limited by people's idiosyncrasies, selfish ideals, issues and phobias, it can place the church in the category of smallness. Wherever smallness exists in mind, goals and Godly purpose, there is imprisonment or the possibility of imprisonment, regardless of the size of the church. It is my prayer that through these writings awareness and enlightenment will come to this devastating quagmire that plagues many of our churches. Primarily, that is in my experience, of the small local church. This is so that we will no longer continue to be or in danger of being **The Church Held Hostage.**

Chapter I

The Beginning of My Lesson

In the year of 1996, in the month of July, I was called to be the pastor of the Memorial Baptist Church. The church was located at 19 - 21 Magnolia St. in the city of Newark NJ at that time. It appeared to be a nice small church with a whole lot of potential. I was very impressed by the inner appearance of the sanctuary. It let me know that someone had been hard at work. The late Rev. Bonney, the previous pastor, had been called home to be with our Lord in that same year a few months earlier. I was 33 years of age by that time with a young family. I was married with three children. My first born, Alfred Jr. was

13, my second born, Clarysha was 11, and the youngest Christopher was 8 years old. I was extremely ambitious and full of life and expectations for the church and my new ministerial responsibility. I'd planned on using at my disposal all the gifts and abilities bestowed to me by our wonderful Savior's Spirit to take the Memorial Baptist Church to a greater level under my leadership. It was my goal and my intention to build on the foundation of my forerunners and take Memorial to a new plateau. After all, I came from a well taught church and good leadership. I had the example of a good pastor, the Rev. Willie W. Wilson, and working strategies. My home church, the Mount Calvary Baptist Church in Jersey City, NJ, was an active church that in many ways functioned as a well oiled machine. Adding to that, I'd become active in that ministry. I was a part of many of the ministries in the church. I participated in the music ministry as lead and bass guitarist, with the choirs as director and at time leading songs. I taught and participated in various classes and served as the assistant to the pastor, just to name a few. I worked and fellowshipped well with the deacons and the other church officers. Because I knew that my ministry consisted of more than the pulpit, I was willing to work where I was needed. I wanted to bring all these experiences with me. It was not my intention to transform the Memorial Baptist Church into another Mount Calvary Baptist Church, but it was my intention to enhance Memorial. It was my desire, and I believed the vision which God the Almighty had given me, to do great things at and with the church. But I was in for a rude awakening. I was not aware of what laid ahead. There was a spirit and a mentality that had gained a strong hold on the church. This hold had no intention of letting go, but appeared to gain momentum down through the years. There was a spirit of complacency as well as an unwillingness to grow. There was a satisfaction of remaining that size or minimizing the growth of the church. I didn't realize it at the time and it has taken me about 11 years or so to obtain some type of understanding that the church had been in a hostage position. I am and have been in war against this spirit and mentality for most of my pastorate. It was only in the recent year or so that I've been enlightened to why. For many times I've questioned my ability to pastor. Many times I doubted myself critically. Many times I've viewed myself as a failure, and felt like giving up. I know that there are many things I could and should have done differently. I know that there was much more I could have and should have done. But to say that the church would have been where I'd hoped, in all honesty, it is hard to say. But I do believe that some things would have been different. I found consolation in the fact that I was not alone. I've learned down through the years that those who were before me enter the pastorate position with like passion and enthusiasm as I. They worked diligently and unselfishly to lead the church in the direction they were moved by the Spirit to go. But they too had to deal with this hostage spirit that got a hold to the church. For had they been able to truly achieve all what was in their heart to do, the church would have possibly been much further than it was. I may have walked into a church of mega proportions. I dare not say, in any wise, that they failed, because they did not. Not by a long shot. For to say that they failed, is to say that God failed and God will never fail. So much has been accomplished through their efforts and leadership. I'm grateful to the Lord Jesus Christ that there still remains a remnant of the leaders, as well as people who can witness of the struggles and successes of their leadership. I was informed that only two others, prior to myself, was pastor for a significant number of years. The Rev. Bennett Johnson, who pastors the Greater Mount Moriah Baptist Church in Newark NJ and the late Rev. C.F. Bonney were pastors there for about 8 years each. All others in between pastorates were brief. I also found consolation in my fellow pastors and other congregations. They let me know that many churches are in the same struggle. But most of all I thank God that I've found encouragement in the Holy Scriptures. The apostles continued to encourage the New Testament churches through times of mayhem and manipulation tactics. I've often wondered 'why the struggle Lord?' Every time it appeared that the church was on the move, it seemed like the bottom would fall out. So many times I had to battle the spirit of jealousy when I saw other ministries growing, while at the same time it was hard to keep the bills of the church paid. Many times I had to forfeit monetary gifts I should have received from the church in order for the church to meet its obligations. Some times that wasn't enough. I've had to sacrifice paying my own bills in an effort to help the financial situation of the church. So often and even now I fight frustration, disappointment, and feelings of inadequacy as a pastor. But I've come to terms with the purpose of these ministerial struggles. As unpleasant and uncomfortable as it was and can be, the Lord had to let me experience these dilemmas for His glory and to gain this information. As Joseph proclaimed in the scriptures, I also echo the same sentiment *What was meant for evil, God meant for good.* The Spirit of the Almighty God, informed me that these situations are for the benefit of letting other pastors and small churches know, who are also in the struggle, that you are not alone in your battles against these wrong spirits at work in the church. It wasn't then or is it now for me to accept defeat, but to expose the problem and let others, who are still struggling as I and the Memorial Baptist Church, know that faithfulness in spite of the conditions will be rewarded by God. <u>For the race is not given to the swift, neither the battle to the strong but to the one who endureth to the end.</u> The Memorial Baptist Church is currently located at 355 -357 14th Ave., in the city of Newark NJ. We are presently experiencing a period of endurance and purging as well as a period of preparation for God's movement and blessings. For the Scripture says in Galatians 6:9; <u>"And let us not be weary in well- doing: for in due season we shall reap, if we faint not."</u> Therefore, I am confident that when the Lord is ready, He can and He will move mightily at the Memorial Baptist Church. Romans 8:31; <u>"What shall we then say to these things? If God be for us, who can be against us?"</u> So for those who are enduring what I and the church are enduring, be encouraged. As the scripture says, 1 Corinthians 15: 58; <u>"Therefore, my beloved brethren, be ye steadfast, unmovable, always abounding in the work of the Lord; forasmuch as ye know that your labor is not in vain in the Lord."</u>

Chapter II

The Plight of the Small Local Church

There are many small local churches being held hostage. Those which are not currently in this condition are in danger of being held in a hostage position. It may be unpopular to say and an unfortunate situation to be in, but there are many churches being held hostage. How is this accomplished? In the small local church most of the work done is done on a voluntary basis. When people who don't share the vision that has been given to the angel of the church, who is the pastor, by the Lord Jesus Christ, who is the head of the church, it can put the church in a hostage position. Not sharing the vision doesn't necessarily mean working against the leadership only, but also not working at all. Some people in the church have their own vision for the church, which at times differ drastically from the Pastor's vision, while others want to take a neutral position. People will use tactics of intimidation and threats of membership relocation, either spoken directly to the pastor or spoken to others in the church of what they will do if things don't go their way. I must say that it is extremely important for people to have the opportunity to share their concerns and ideas about the church. Everyone in the church should and must have a voice. But unless there are biblical dialogs as well as understanding that what we do is for the promulgation and edification of the kingdom of God, our own agendas will supersede God's agenda. Plus, there are some people in the church that just do not put in as much enthusiasm in working for the church. Because in all honesty there is either no salary involved, or the financial stipend is minimal. Some people do what they do for what they can get out of it. It must be understood that we are to communicate with each other in a rational and loving manner.

I thank God that in every church there is what I call the faithful few. These are the members of the congregation who are dedicated and sincere concerning their church. These are the ones that make the sacrifices needed for the church to move on. It is on the backs of the faithful few that the small churches primarily operate. It is the dedication of the willing workers that support the continuation of the small branches of Zion. I thank God for the faithful few that exist in all of our churches who share the vision with the God appointed leaders. Thank God for the prayers of the faithful few.

Chapter III

What is a hostage situation?

I'm sure that a general concept of <u>what is a hostage</u> exists in the minds of many people. But for clarity and support of this concept as it relates to the church, it would be to our advantage to view the definition of the word in order to substantiate how it relates to the small church dilemma. What is a hostage situation? The word hostage is defined as followed.

Hostage / hos·tage

hos·tage [hóstij] (plural hos·tages) n
1. captive held for ransom: somebody held prisoner by a person or group, for example, a criminal or a terrorist organization, until certain demands are met or money is handed over
2. Somebody manipulated by another: a person or group of people whose freedom of action is restricted or controlled by a more powerful organization by implied threats or other means
3. Security or pledge: a person or thing given or held as security (archaic) [13th century. From Old French (h) ostage, from late Latin obsidiatus "hostageship," literally "sitting in the way of," from, ultimately, sedere "to sit."] a hostage to fortune a remark or action that could potentially lead to trouble or difficulty and so is better avoided

Encarta ® World English Dictionary © & (P) 1998- 2004 Microsoft Corporation. All rights reserved.

How are hostage situations created?

There are at least 3 ways hostage situations are created.

1. By power play
2. By manipulation
3. By inferiority complex

1. By Power Play

One way that creates a hostage situation is when a person or group of people overpower another person or group of people and hold them against their will. When an individual or team (the hostage holder or holders) manifest strength and gain control over another individual or team (the hostage or hostages), the hostage or hostages become subject to the will and authority of the holder or holders. The hostage or hostages become the prisoner and /or slave to the holder.

How does this relate to the church?

The way this situation relates to the church is by people who are very forceful and loudly opinionated. There are people in the church that have gained positions of power and intimidate others in the church, either to support their agenda or not stand against them. I faced a few situations at Memorial from people who had positions of power and didn't want to compromise for the growth and well being of the church. They were very insistent on implementing their agenda. They would do or say what they felt necessary to force others to back them or to back down.

2. By Manipulation

Another way that creates a hostage situation is through manipulation. It is also possible to create a hostage situation when a person or group is manipulated, tricked, deceived into believing that the holder has a weapon or has power at their disposal that they don't actually have.

How does it relate to the church?

The way in which this situation relates to the church is when people in the church capitalize on the fears, weaknesses and concerns other members have in the church and manipulate them. When a person feels overlook, under appreciated or betrayed by someone in the church, rather it's by the pastor, officers, or other people, the manipulator communicates with them in a way to further fuel the problem rather than attempt to put out the fire. Once they believe that the door is open for their foolish ideals, they will attempt to influence people in order to promote their program. This type will attempt to convince other members that they are one of the few in the church that knows what should be done. This type tries to convince others that their way, that is the manipulator, is the best way. They too will say and do whatever they deem necessary to get their way.

Another way manipulators operate is by gaining the confidence of others, persuading them of their false love for the church. There are people who profess love for God, the pastor and the church and try to project the image of concern. But truthfully they are primarily concerned about their own agenda. They camouflage their selfish idealism under the covers of love. Love is not one sided. If they truly loved their church and their pastor, they would be cooperative and instrumental in helping the church come together. Their intention would be a desire for the growth of God's kingdom, the growth of the church at large and its well being.

3. By an Inferiority Complex

Another way that a hostage situation is created is by the weakness of a person or group of people. When one believes that they are inferior to another.

How does it relate to the church?

This situation relates to the church when people believe they have little or nothing to offer God's program. Some, I believe, are intimidated by the talents and the abilities of others. When they compare themselves and their abilities to others, they may quite possibly feel that what they have is not good enough to participate in the program. I believe for this reason they are reluctant to participate in the church. Many will not testify, sing or serve because secretly they may possess feelings of inadequacy.

Chapter IV

The Perpetrators and How They Perpetrate.

The perpetrators holding the small church hostage consist of at least two groups of people. Both, no doubt, will insist that they are not guilty of this act, but unfortunately, they are. One group performs this directly and the other indirectly. One set does this intentionally, while the others do it ignorantly. In other words, some know exactly what they are doing, while the others may not be fully aware of what they are doing. Rather it is the pastor, deacons, deaconesses, clerks, secretaries, trustees, musicians, choir directors, choir members, teachers or any positions needed and useful, they can be perpetrators. There are various ministries necessary in the church for it to function as it should. One person can't do it all. In a church with a small congregation it becomes necessary for people to do more than one job. Even when ministerial activity decreases, having multiple church responsibilities still exist. In most cases, the smaller the amount of people, the more hats have to be worn by the same people. There are some parishioners who do what they do for the love of God and the Lord Jesus, their church and their pastor. But unfortunately, some people do what they do to gain power and position in the church. It would be beneficial if it were done for the right reason and with a healthy attitude. But when a church becomes reliant on people with the wrong attitude and selfish motives, they become or are at risk of being hostage to them. They make an effort to show some people how valuable they are and the church can't do without them. These people have developed the mentality that the church can't function without them. They have the mentality that if I don't do it, then it won't get done. Unfortunately, in some aspects, they are right. At times, in order to prove their point, they won't do their duty so people will recognize what they do in the church. They shun their responsibility because they are in position to hold the church hostage. One of two things will happen. Either someone else will have to take on additional responsibilities, or the work must go undone. How the perpetrators can hold the church hostage is by the following:

1. Those who are not concerned about fulfilling their duties adequately and efficiently because they believe they can't be replaced, simply because there's no one to take their place.

Over the years as pastor, I have dealt with people who were in positions in title only. There are people in the church that hold positions and titles who are not fulfilling their duty. They hadn't made an effort to improve because of their belief that no one is there to take their spot. To reiterate what was said earlier, most of the work done in the small local church is done voluntarily. Because there's no salary paid to people for their work, it becomes difficult to pressure them who aren't fulfilling their obligations. I served as the Shop Steward and alternate steward of my union for a number of years at my place of employment. I often shared with those in management and the union that I understand both parties' perspectives. When I'm at the job, I have people over me. When I'm at the church, I have people under me. But the advantage they possess that I don't is monetary. If one doesn't do their job, they can be suspended or terminated. But at church, people who are working voluntarily, if they are pressured, can chose not to work or leave the church.

2. Those that are afraid to teach someone else for fear they will be replaced.

There are people in the church that use ignorance to hold the church hostage. When others are ignorant in reference to the function of an office and ministry, the person or people in that office and ministry can secure their positions.

3. Not knowing what or how to teach because they have not taken the time to be taught themselves.

There are people in the church occupying offices that refuse to increase their knowledge and improve their ability to operate better in their office. They are reluctant to teach someone else because in all honesty, they can't teach something they don't know themselves. They also can't teach, if they don't know how. A genuine effort to teach, in my opinion, is not made for fear of discovering their limited knowledge of their office. As long as it appears that they know what they are doing, no one will make an effort to have them replaced.

4. *Those who want a lot of praise*

There are people in the church that want to be acknowledged for everything they do. They have a passionate desire to be praised for their work. There's nothing wrong, at least in my opinion, with wanting to be appreciated and recognized in the church for the work one does. It is a great motivator when someone compliments you. It's a good feeling. It gives you a sense of accomplishment. But when being recognized is your only motive, it becomes a problem. For some reason, people feel as though they must compete for God's attention as well as the pastor's and their fellow brothers and sisters in Christ. They must be praised above every one or at least in the upper percentage. If they don't receive the praise and recognition they believe they're entitled to, they hop to another church or threaten to do so.

5. *Those in the churches that don't want responsibility and don't want to be taught.*

There are some people in the church that don't want the responsibility of ministerial participation. If they have no responsibilities at the church, then they believe they can come and go as they please without guilt of abandonment.

People also use ignorance as an excuse for their lack of being responsible in the church. They have somehow been convinced that a lack of knowledge will pardon them from kingdom duty. I believe that it's one of the major reasons why people won't come out for teaching nor do they study. The old adage that what I don't know can't hurt me roams the mind like a bad habit. What many people inside and outside the church may not be aware of is this truth. There are not only sins of commission but also sins of omission. James 4:17 says, "Therefore to him that knoweth to do good, and doeth it not, to him it is sin."

Attitudes that contributes to the problem

Doubt

Inconsistency

Unfaithfulness

Selfishness

Lack of giving

No conviction

Chapter V

The Disadvantage of a Small Congregation.

In this chapter we'll explore the difficulties related with having a small congregation. As we stated earlier pertaining to situations and circumstances beyond people's control, these and other predicaments impose obstacles on the church. Having a small congregation presents a number of challenges and difficulties. Because of the limited quantity of people, it makes it hard and almost impossible to be about the type of ministry many pastors desire. Why? It is extremely necessary for people to participate and contribute to the ministry. The mandate of the church is the spreading of the Gospel of God's saving grace through Jesus Christ and ministering to the needs of the less fortunate. We are commissioned by Jesus Christ <u>to minister to the poor, fatherless, widows, disabled and the sick.</u> Without adequate contributions and participation, it's difficult to be about that mandate. It becomes overwhelming to the small church when only a few attempt to do the work of the church. I've expressed to the church, which I pastor, for many years that a church should not exist just for itself. All too often, some missions have to be put on the back burner due to at least three reasons: people, places and money. Because it's impossible to be multiple places at one time, perform multiple tasks at one time and have inadequacy of funds, some things have to wait or be dismissed. To add insult to injury, there are aspects in life that can't be helped nor avoided. There are circumstances of life which presents aspects in life that affect us. There are occasions when these circumstances are used by some as excuses for their lack of participation and attendance in church. When one is honest about these situations that arise, they have a legitimate excuse. It then isn't used by people to hold the church hostage. It's just a reality of life that can't be helped. One of these circumstances is sickness. When members of the congregation become truly ill and have medical problems, it affects the small church greatly. It's not my intention to minimize the value of one's membership in a large congregation nor to say that their absence is not recognized, but it is recognized and felt at a greater extent with a smaller congregation.

Another one of these circumstances in life that can't be avoided is death. When members depart from this life to be with our Lord, the smaller church congregations are greatly affected, especially if those members were essential parts of that church. The dilemma is made worse when the congregation is dying off, but no one is coming in to fill the void. It's harmful to a small church when the pews are becoming vacant by sickness and death. The spirit is willing but the flesh is weak. Sickness and death just can't be helped nor avoided. They are circumstances in life and of life that will take place.

Besides sickness and death, the Bible also speaks in **2Timothy 2:3** of the time when there will be a great falling away from the church. Although this falling away will affect many churches, it's seen and felt at a greater magnitude when it happens in the small local churches.

There are additional factors that create problems with church attendance. These factors are used by some as excuses to mask a lack of dedication. Although there are legitimate reasons given by parishioners for their absence, some quite often are not sincere or truthful.

People have used the weather as an excuse. Some have used sickness, finances, family emergencies, personal struggles, tiredness and whatever else they believe will be accepted as an excuse. But the ironies of these excuses are that they don't hinder the same people when it comes to other activities. It's strange that the same excuse that prevents someone from going to church won't stop them from going other places. People do what they want to do. If church isn't on their primary "to do" list, it will take the back seat quite often. But on many occasions when I'm feeling weak and tired and unable to do what I'm commissioned to do for the Lord, I remember that the joy of the Lord is my strength. Remember, **the Lord wants results, not excuses.**

The struggles of Small memberships.

Another aspect that places the small church at a disadvantage is a low membership. Where there is a small membership, there is the potential of what we will call the *"LL"* factor; less and limits. This LL factor places the church in a hostage predicament or at greater risk of being held hostage.

The "LL" factor:

One way that the church is held hostage through the "LL" factor is by its finances. Low membership creates difficulties in raising adequate financial resources. This factor creates difficult challenges in several ways. It is already enough of a challenge to raise adequate funds for ministry with a small congregation. But when these factors interfere with the process, it increases the level of difficulty in accomplishing that goal.

1. <u>When people are reluctant to tithe and give generously in offerings</u>

In the first year of my pastorate at Memorial, I did my best to increase the revenue of the church by asking the congregation to pay tithes and give just a little more. I was met with a great reluctance by some of the church officers. They insisted that the amount which I was trying to raise could not be done. I shared with them information about a few churches I knew, who were even smaller in number than we were. One church in particular averaged about $2,000.00 or more per week. Their general offering alone was over $600.00. Whenever members are satisfied with the small amounts they give, believing they are giving enough, it activates the "LL" factor.

2. When people are unable to give generously because of their own personal financial troubles and limitations;

When parishioners are currently or begin to struggle with their own finances, it hinders them from giving. One of two things happen. Either they are hesitant to give or they decrease in the amount that they give. In this case, they are now being held hostage by their own financial predicament. Until they break free from that imprisonment through faith, such as the woman in scripture with the two mites, improvements in their financial situation, or decrease in their financial obligations, they will not give any more than what they are giving. It takes faith to give generously.

3. When there is a lack of desire to give toward the ministry.

There are people in the church who simply choose to limit their contributions to the church. They attempt to hide their lack of desire to give behind a mountain of excuses such as: *'I have my own bills to pay; the money is going into somebody's pocket; I've got better things to do with my money; the pastor will get it'* and so on and so on. In the book of Malachi 3: 8, God asks the question *will a man rob God?* And the answer returned *"Yes. Through tithes and offerings."*

Other problems caused by the "LL" factor.

In many cases where there is low membership, there is low revenue. This hinders other necessary ministries from being implemented. Finances are very important in order to be about ministry.

Social programs:

The church has been given its agenda by Jesus through scripture to take care of the widows, fatherless children, and the disabled. Unfortunately because of limits in finances, every church will not be able to fulfill this mandate; at least not on their own. There are people who are in desperate need of help. I'm not talking about those who just want a hand out and no effort to change their situation. But I'm talking about those who are making a genuine effort to do right by their families as well as for themselves. Sometimes all they need is a hand making ends meet. In my 12 years of pastorate at the Memorial Baptist Church, as I previously mentioned, I've often shared with the congregation that a church should not exist just for itself, but for the community and the cause of Christ.

Voices that residents and politicians won't hear:

If there is one thing in life that I've come to understand, it is that there is strength in numbers. Numbers attract politicians and residents. Large numbers get attention. In reference to the political arena, I believe that politicians respect two things. It's difficult for the pastor of a small congregation to be taken as seriously by politicians as we should. I understand that many politicians are looking for one of two things, or a combination of two things. These two things are simply dollars and votes. I doubt very seriously politicians will admit this, but in all honesty, if it appears that the congregation can't produce an adequate amount of money and/or votes, they become the least to be heard.

In the community it's hard to have a great impact because enough attention might not be drawn because of the low number of congregates. It is harder to get police presence and political input when secretly a small church may not be viewed as a political asset. Once again I don't want to be misunderstood. God is able to do more with a dedicated few than an undedicated multitude. He can move politicians and communities. If we as a church get on one accord and rise above the quagmire of petty selfish issues, God can and will still use the small church mightily.

Church participation:

Having a small congregation makes it hard to remove the perpetrators who are holding the church hostage. This is simply because the pool of replacements comes from the congregation. If there is no one in the congregation willing to serve in any church ministry or if there is no one else to select from, the perpetrators can and will remain in power. In that case the church remains hostage. Some additional affects of lack of attendance will be discussed in the next chapter.

Chapter VI

How Absenteeism Harms the Small Congregation Church

Absenteeism is another way in which the church is being held hostage. When members are absent from an already small congregation, it can have both short and long term affects. I'm not quite sure whether or not people understand the magnitude of how their absenteeism affects the church. At times I wonder do some of the congregation even care. I pray that the absence is due to ignorance of its affects and not of uncaring hearts. But unfortunately, all too often I've seen evidence of what appears to be uncaring hearts by many. To those who are in the category of lack of understanding the magnitude of absence, as well as those who seem not to care, I will attempt to enlighten and explain to you the affects. Hopefully and prayerfully uncaring attitudes will be transformed, hearts will be changed and there will be a re-evaluation of perspectives.

(1.) It's very disheartening and discouraging for a pastor to look over the congregation and see a host of vacant seats. It is in my opinion equivalent to a person planning a nice gathering, preparing food, prepare places to sit, going all out, only to have little or no people show up. Many pastors are very reluctant to express their disappointments when they see vacant pews. Because in some way, shape or form, it leads us to question the effectiveness of our preaching and leadership. It leads us to wonder if we are reaching anyone. We preach to reach. That's our calling and our responsibility. Although we know that God is in control, we must still deal with real human emotions. Let's be real with this. I know how it feels when people are not coming to church, let alone, not joining. When the pews are empty, who's here to be reached? When there are vacant seats then who are we reaching? We continue to persevere because of the fire burning within us like

Jeremiah. <u>Jeremiah 20:9 "Then I said, I will not make mention of Him, nor speak any more in His name. But His word was in mine heart as a burning fire shut up in my bones, and I was weary with forbearing, and I could not stay."</u> This disappointment isn't restricted to Sunday morning worship only, but it includes bible study, prayer meeting, Sunday school and other events as well. Not only do we preach to reach, we teach to reach also. Some pastors are guilty of inflating their membership number and down playing their struggles with ministry and growth when talking to others. This is simply because numbers translate in the minds of many to an appearance of a successful ministry. No pastor wants or anticipates their ministry projecting an appearance of ineffectiveness, unproductiveness and meaninglessness. One of the many reasons why pastors seek other churches to pastor is because the churches where they are may be currently held hostage and appears to have no desire to break free.

(2.) When people are absent from church, not only does it dishearten and discourage the pastor, but it also disheartens and discourages other church members. I believe that anyone who is about growth and productivity wants and seeks to be connected with something productive, meaningful, effective and fulfilling. In all honesty, we love to talk and some will even brag at times of how well their church is doing. But when people don't show up, congregants begin to look elsewhere for a congregation who is like-minded concerning church growth and mission. It is extremely difficult to get a ministry to be about something when people won't show up. I recall numerous occasions when guest would come to visit looking for someone, only for that person not to be there themselves. Members become reluctant to attend church because many will say that no one is coming anyway. Parishioners won't attend pray meeting, bible study and other events as well because they believe no one will attend. This is the primary reason why they should attend. For if everyone in the church will think this way the church would then be completely empty.

(3.) Absenteeism also cast a negative image about the church to visitors. Let's face the facts. People visit churches for at least two reasons. I'm not talking about those who come merely looking for a handout and not a hand up. I'm not talking about those who come attempting to get over on the church. I'm talking about those who attend searching for a church home and/or support someone. Either they come to share with family and friends or they are looking for a church home. As I fore stated, anyone who is about growth and productivity wants and seeks to be connected with something productive, meaningful, effective and fulfilling.

If the church appears to have poor attendance, it can cause visitors and potential new members to question what the church is about. It is something completely different if it is a new born, up-coming church. But if that church has been on the scene for a significant amount of time, it generates questions about its lack of growth.

(4.) Church officers and leaders can hold the church hostage by absenteeism. Officers' and leaders' absenteeism causes a hindrance in church work. With a small congregation, as was mentioned previously in this book, multiple ministries can mean multiple responsibilities for the same people. When a person agrees to participate in ministry, primarily as an officer, there exist the potential of them holding the church hostage by absenteeism. They harm the church because either someone else will have to take on extra responsibilities or the work is left undone.

(5.) Absenteeism harms the church finances. As was mentioned previously, having a small congregation places extra pressure on the contributing parishioners.

Low membership already creates great difficulty in raising adequate financial resources. The "LL" factor is already activated by low membership. When you add in absenteeism, the financial well being of the church is severely threatened. When the small church frequently deals with an absentee problem, much needed offerings are absent as well. Lest I'm misunderstood, I want to make it crystal clear that the church is not about money, but the church needs money to function. It is amazing to me how people are under the impression that the church can operate without money or very little of it. It is harmful to a church's finances when members are absent, but it would be helpful if parishioners would attempt to make up for the times of their absence financially. The small church will fare much better if people understood and cared that they should either give tithes and offerings when they return from their absence or give before a planned absence if possible. The congregants need to know that the financial obligations of the church continue even when they are not present.

(6) People who are not faithful in their attendance are less likely to invite other people to come to church. People who are not dedicated to their church are less likely to be

dedicated in assisting where needed for church growth. When it comes to the harm absenteeism contributes to the small congregations, I believe that some are not aware while there are others who **just don't care.**

Which one are you?

Chapter VII

The Advantages of the Small Local Church

The small local church has a great opportunity to demonstrate the sustaining power of God. For the greatest victory and the most impressive victory comes not from them that are expected to win, but from them who are expected to lose. God gets glory by the triumphs He gives to those others desire to fail and expect to fail. On many occasions we, at the Memorial Baptist Church, faced situations that appeared to be insurmountable. In addition to that, there were people inside and outside the church that further complicated matters. I've even had some who wanted me to fail personally as a pastor. But God manifested His awesomeness and sustained us. When finances weren't available and the bank accounts were overdrawn, bills had to be paid and repairs had to be made, when it looked bleak, at those moments were God's greatest opportunity to show the haters and the spectators that He is God. The advantage that the small local church possesses is the opportunity to demonstrate and operate in faith. When we praise and worship the God of our salvation, in spite of what the situations appear to be, God is magnified.

Another advantage of the small church is the capacity to accomplish what a mega-church will have great difficulty accomplishing. Because of the mass of people that occupy their huge structures and arenas, it creates the tough task of doing what a small church has the possibility of doing. That accomplishment is a sense of closeness. I recall some of the lyrics of a TV sitcom name Cheers. The location was a small local bar where people would go for drinks and chatting. *"You want to go where everybody knows your name."* It is very difficult for everyone to know everyone's name in a mega-church. There may and will be some that will stand out, such as:

the Pastor, the Chairperson of a board, a lead singer or director. In other words, it would be no doubt someone in the spotlight. But the chances of that person in the spotlight knowing everybody, let alone knowing them on more than an, *"I recognize the face basis,"* is slim. Even the Pastor, unless he possesses some type of special ability, will not be able to remember everyone's name. It is easier for a hundred people to remember one face than it is for one person to remember a hundred faces. The small church have a great opportunity to function in unity, exemplify a sense of family, and the personal one on one attention many desire to have in their church.

Another advantage is the glory in growth. We must all be reminded that every large church and mega-ministry started from a small group of people. It was through the Holy Spirit's intervention, prayers and willingness of the congregants to witness and the Lord adding to the church which caused the church to grow. Although every church can't be mega in size, they all can be mega in heart, faith, love, compassion, responsibility and mercy in the work of the kingdom.

One more advantage that the small church possesses is lowered expectations from critics. People tend to expect more from the larger and mega-churches. Because of their large attendance, greater financial revenue is expected to be generated as well as social ministries preformed. It is almost always easier to assume that the pastor and some of the staff are somehow on the take, especially when the pastor possesses fine clothes, cars and eats well. People assume that church revenue is being diverted into the pastor's pockets or someone else's. Many fail to understand that those serving in the pastorate are blessed through the congregation. People will criticize and say that the pastor and others are getting the money. They look for big things to be done by the larger and mega-churches for the community, both socially and financially.

The small churches, although we possess the desire and intent to minister to our communities and our congregants with more than just scriptural encouragement, are in many cases unable to do so at the level we want. I myself would love to have ministries that feed, shelter, clothe and assist people greater than what we have already done. I know for myself pastors who share the same sentiment. Having a small congregation diverts and hinders critics from bad mouthing the church, because in some way, shape or form, there is less expected.

Chapter VIII

Heading toward Liberty from hostage ship

In this chapter we will explore some options for breaking the hostage cycle. The enemy has no intentions on letting it be easy for us to spread the gospel messege of God's saving grace. The devil is trying his best to stop people from receiving the message of God's love. Satan don't want us to tell of Jesus' sacrificial death for our sins. Because of that sacrificial death, God is willing to forgive our sins. If he can keep the church, large and small, filled with ungodly and unprofitable issues, he can hinder the spread of the gospel. If he can get our minds focused on the questions and not the answer, than he can disrupt the movement of God in our lives and in the world. These are the practices we've begun to implement at the church. I've learned down through the years that nothing can work without cooperation and participation. Although we are still in a struggle, I have witnessed areas of improvement in the church. I know that the reason why we have been in the struggle for as long as we have is because there has been a lack of cooperation and participation. As in any relationship, it takes more than one for it to thrive as a unit. I dare not try to cast the blame of our struggle on others. I have my part. There are some things I could have and should have done differently. There were some things that I implemented to soon, some I didn't implement soon enough, and others I didn't implement at all. My reasons for not doing so at those times were out of fear and concern of upsetting people. But I've learned the hard way that sometimes it's necessary to make people a little uncomfortable in order for the church to be what it needs to be. The greater the cooperation, the more the church will be liberated from hostage ship. I say this because, my home church, the Mount Calvary Baptist Church, emerged from a situation of a church on the verge of closing to a position of respect not only from the religious community, but the secular community as well. Although I realize it was due to God, but it was also people who came and joined the church with the drive to work and was willing to hear God. They followed leadership and worked diligently in what they were asked to do and they did it to the best of their abilities. They served in multiple offices and taught others as they came in. Many of those which came in developed a desire to learn. Those workers tried their best to do what was necessary for the cause of Christ and the well being of the church. Because money was low at times, things were done with an effort to keep cost at a minimum. Men came together to do repairs, women came together to beautify the church and many came together to work for the growth of the church. If the small churches are going to grow, or at the least, sustain a decent level of functionality, there must be willing participants.

1. *First understanding God's order and design for the church. Who's in charge?*

Jesus proclaims in Matthew 16:18......"upon this rock I will build my church"...........

On many occasions we must be reminded that Jesus is the head of the church. Eph. 5:23 "For the husband is the head of the wife, even as Christ is the head of the church: He is the savior of the body."

Col. 1:18 "And He is the head of the body, the church: who is the beginning, the firstborn from the dead; that in all things He might have the pre-eminence." There is an order established by God for the church.

Next, the pastor is the under shepherd and is held responsible by God and to God for the people in the church. Heb. 13:7 "Remember them which have the rule over you, who have spoken unto you the word of God: whose faith follow, considerating the end of their conversation."

Heb.13:17 "Obey them that have the rule over you, and submit yourselves: for they watch for your souls, as they that must give an account, that they may do it with joy, and not with grief: for that is unprofitable for you."

2. *Operating in faith*

The Bible says in 2 Corinthians 5: 7 "For we walk by faith and not by sight."

Also in Hebrews 11:1; "Now faith is the substance of things hoped for, the evidence of things not seen."

It is vitally necessary to the small church to keep faith in focus. It is extremely challenging to operate by faith when it appears that conditions in the church are overwhelming struggles. I've come to realize that faith by some has been reduced to the mere concept of believing that God will do for us what we want Him to do. I agree that it takes faith. Jesus said throughout the gospels when someone came for healing and deliverance the words *"your faith have made you whole".* But how faith is defined in its original language takes us far beyond just getting from God what we desire. Some concepts of faith's operation comes very close to making God appear as a genie from the lamp. When you examine the concept of faith in the Greek, faith comes from the word *pistis* which means belief, trust and confidence. So faith is not only believing that God can do and God will do, but also confidence in His ability, i.e., God knows what He is doing. We must trust God even when the outcomes of situations appear not to be in our favor. Confidence in God is the only way we will be able to endure. "…Faith without works is dead…" James 2: 26

3. *What we prayer for*

Since God established the church in Jesus, Jesus Himself being the head of the church and having set the order of it, it goes without saying that we pray to the Father in His name for guidance. It is through prayer that we communicate with God and He with us. Prayer is the spoken communication between God and man. But just as prayer is essential to the well being of the small church, what we pray for is also essential. There have been many times I've prayed to the Lord for strength to lead, as well as knowledge to lead. But I've learned also that it is important to pray for help to lead. It matters not how strong nor how knowledgeable a pastor may be, no one can do it all alone. We need in all our churches people who are willing to help in the church. Help does not necessarily mean that people have to be in leadership positions, but assisting in areas where needed.

I've also learned that it is necessary to pray for membership increase. The Bible says in James 4: 2, in the later portion of that verse, …."yet ye have not, because ye ask not." It is not demeaning to the church or to the pastor to pray for more members. For it is the will of God that man should be saved as well as church and kingdom growth. I've had moments when I've questioned whether or not the condition of the church would improve. I've had my share of doubts. So at those moments I would pray for assurance of His presence and a sign that the church will endure. I had to earnestly ask God in my time of weakness to show me something which will keep me or re-motivate me.

It is additionally important that the church congregants pray for the church and pastor when they are outside the church as well as inside the church.

4. *Dedication and Sacrifice*

Essential to any and every organization and institution's growth and productivity are dedication and sacrifice. People in the church, from the pulpit to the pews, must maintain a sense of duty and responsibility. Anything that is and will be done for God, the church and the kingdom must involve dedication and sacrifice. In order for a person to be dedicated, there must be a willingness to sacrifice and one will not be willing to sacrifice unless there is dedication. As was referred to earlier, having a small congregation will place congregants in the position of undertaking more responsibility. This translates to doing in spite of one's personal circumstances and feelings. It means that you have to go even when you don't feel like going. It means that you have to fulfill your obligation regardless.

5. *Overcoming fear of shrinkage*

If the truth be shared, those of us who pastor have a great concern about losing members. Deep within those of us that has low memberships are the feelings of fear and concerns that there might be further shrinkage of our already small congregations. Not only do the pastor deal with this fear, but also caring members of the church. Because this concern exists in the minds of people, the people who want to control the church and hold the church hostage will use this to their advantage. But we must be confident in the sustaining power of God. I've learned that sometimes there must be a decrease before there can be an increase. Sometimes God will expose and weed out the trouble makers that He may prepare the church for growth and power. God has proven to me that He can and will take care of His.

6. *Outreach programs and Evangelism -*

What many of our small churches need to help overpower the forces which holds the church hostage is new blood. Who's needed in the church are new members. But not just anybody, but people who share the vision of the leader, who loves the Lord and concern about the well being of the church. The small church, as in every church, regardless of the size, needs people that will promote the gospel of Jesus Christ and the growth of their particular church. This is why evangelism is of the utmost importance. There needs to be outreach programs to draw people in the church, primarily to people without a church home and new converts.

7. *Beware of burning out of the faithful few*

In order for a small church congregation not to experience burnout of the faithful few there must be an understanding and acknowledging of the small church current limitations. I've learned to accept some of the current limitations and try to run the church according to what we can do right now. It is not an effort to limit God, but to hold in consideration the congregation's well being. Burning out the faithful few will add insult to injury in reference to an already challenging situation.

8. *Advice seeking*

I've learned that there are and have been pastors that experienced the hardships of a struggling church. Through the power of God's Holy Spirit and the faithfulness of dedicated parishioners, many small congregations increased to large congregations. New edifices had to be constructed to house the increase of congregants. Larger building were purchased and renovated to accommodate the growth. It is always to pastors' and smaller churches' advantage to gain knowledge from other pastors and churches that have been where others have yet to journey.

9. *Work on getting into key positions to help your congregation economically.*

Because the church operates with funds received from the parishioners, it is absolutely necessary for the people in the church to have means of income. People can't give if they have nothing to give. It is always helpful to a church family for someone to develop connections both religiously and socially that information can be obtained for employment. It is also helpful to a church family for someone to develop connections both religiously and socially that information can be obtained for places of dwelling.

People in our churches and our communities are in need of assistance. Therefore helping those who are in need is helping ourselves.

10. *Stay motivated and encouraged*

Two additional essential aspects needed for overpowering the hostage syndrome are motivation and encouragement. It is of the utmost importance that pastors and devoted congregants maintain a healthy level of motivation and encouragement. In order to focus your attention on that which will produce for the church and the kingdom of God, people must stay in the right frame of mind. It's a great challenge remaining stable in spirit, mind and heart when it appears that the church is just spinning its wheels going nowhere or moving slowly in its purpose. I call it driving on three flat tires. When it seems like this is the situation, it becomes necessary to either repair the tires or replace them. All too often, discouragement, anxiety, frustration, aggravation and just sheer exhaustion can arise. Because of these feelings, it's easy to lose your drive and enthusiasm. But it's always great for motivation to be encouraged by some others who've been there. Remember that God is still in control of it all. God has never failed in showing me that. Because when I faced moments of great despair, I asked the Lord and sometimes pleaded with Him to show me something that I may be motivated and encouraged, and He did. Yes, I know that we walk by faith and not by sight, but the Lord also understands that we are but dust. He knows that every now and then we need a glimpse of the victory set before us, as well as witnesses to verify and speak life into each other. But in addition to that, I also remembered how the Bible says that David encouraged himself in the Lord. Sometimes it requires reaching and searching way, way, way down in your spirit to locate that reserved hope that the Holy Spirit placed in our heart. Romans 8: 28 "And we know that all things work together for good to them that love God, to them who are the called according to His purpose."

The question:

Are you holding the Church hostage?
If you are, it's time to set your hostages free!

Still Learning and Growing:

Even though I've been in the gospel preaching ministry for a little over twenty years and served as pastor for a little over 12 at the time of writing this book, I know that there remains very much to learn. I believe that through these writings many will be blessed. I pray that people who enter into the doors of the church will do so not only with a hunger and thirst for righteousness, but also the drive and motivation to work for the furtherance of the Gospel of Jesus Christ and the growth of the church. I am persuaded that through every trail and every obstacle, God will see me through and that there is a lesson to be abstracted from them. Once again my prayer, as I fore stated, is that awareness and enlightenment will come to this devastating quagmire that plagues many of our churches. Primarily, that is in my experience, that of the small local church. So that we will no longer continue to be or in danger of being **The Church Held Hostage.**

The following is a questionnaire that I've designed for outreach ministry. This survey was designed for the purpose of gaining some idea of how to witness to people who do not currently go to church or do not have a church home.

Outreach Ministry Questionnaire Survey

1. Do you believe that there is a God and Creator?

YES _____
NO _____
I DON'T KNOW_____

2. Do you believe in God?

YES_____
NO _____
I DON'T KNOW_____

If yes, then go on to question number 3.
If no or I don't know, ask the following:

a. Why don't you believe or don't know?

_____

_____

_____

_____

_____

_____

3. Do you believe that God has a plan for this world?

YES_____

NO _____

I DON'T KNOW_____

If no or I don't know, then go on to question number 4.

If yes, ask the following:

a. What do you believe that plan is? _____

_____

_____

_____

_____

4. Do you believe that God has a plan for <u>your life</u>?

YES_____

NO _____

I DON'T KNOW_____

If no or I don't know, ask the following:

a. Why don't you think that God has a plan for your life?

If yes, ask the following:

a. Do you know what that plan is? _____

_____

_____

_____

_____

b. How where you made aware of it? _____

_____

_____

_____

_____

5. If there were someone that you loved so deeply until words could not express how much you loved them, and that person got into so much trouble that it would cost them their lives, and you had the power to help them, would you?

YES_____

NO _____

I DON'T KNOW_____

6. What do you think the condition of the human race is in?_____

_____

_____

_____

_____

_____

7. Do you believe that God loved us so deeply until words could not truly express how much He loved us, and that mankind got into so much trouble that it would cost us our eternal lives, and He had the power to help us, and He did?

YES_____

NO _____

I DON'T KNOW_____

If yes, ask the following:

a. What do you believe God did to help us? _____

_____

_____

_____

8. Do you believe that Jesus is the help that God sent?

YES_____
NO _____
I DON'T KNOW_____

If no, ask the following:
a. Why not?_____

_____

_____

9. Who do you believe that Jesus is? _____

_____

_____

_____

_____

_____

10. Would you be interested in getting to know Him and who He is?

YES_____
NO _____
I DON'T KNOW_____
Maybe_____

11. Do you go to Church?

YES_____
NO _____
Sometimes_____

If no, go to question no. # 12
If yes, ask the following:

a. What is the name of your Church Home? _____

_____

_____

_____

b. How often do you go and what do you participate in?

_____

_____

_____

_____

12. Have you ever gone to Church?

YES_____

NO _____

Sometimes_____

If no, go to the next question 16

If yes, go back to question 11a and 11b, then continue at 13.

13. Did you enjoy it?

YES_____

NO _____

Somewhat_____

14. What about it did you like? _____

_____

_____

_____

_____

_____

15. What about it turned you off?_____

_____

_____

_____

_____

16. If you are searching for a Church home, what are some of the qualities you would look for?

_____

_____

_____

_____

_____

_____

_____

17. If you are not a regular attendee of a Church and want to see what it is all about, what would expect to find?

_____

_____

_____

_____

_____

18. Would you be willing to visit us at our Church?

YES_____

NO _____

Maybe_____

19. Would you be willing to give us an address or some other way of making contact with you to send you information about our Church and coming events?

YES_____

NO _____

Maybe_____

Name(s): _____

_____

_____

_____

_____

_____

_____

_____

Address or Contact

Information:_____

Prayer request:

_____

We thank you so kindly for taking the time to help us reach people for the Kingdom of God in Jesus Christ, our Lord and Savior.

Pastor Alfred A. Dingle Sr. and the
Memorial Baptist Church Family

AD Ministries

11/ 29/2008
12/11/2008
2/ 10 / 2009